MENTAL HEALTH:

Overcoming the inner beast, and a guide towards mental serenity

By

Dr. Kennedy Godson

Copyright @ 2022 Dr. Kennedy Godson

TABLE OF CONTENT

INTRODUCTION

Our emotional, psychological, and social well-being are all parts of our mental health. It influences our thoughts, emotions, and behaviors. Additionally, it influences how we respond to stress, interact with others, and make good decisions. Every period of life, from childhood and adolescence to maturity, is vital for mental health.

Both physical and mental health are crucial aspects of overall health. For instance, depression raises the danger of many different physical health issues, especially chronic diseases like diabetes, heart disease, and stroke. In a similar vein, having chronic illnesses raises your likelihood of developing mental disease.

CHAPTER 1

Types of mental health problems

1. Anger

We all experience anger occasionally; it's just part of being human. Anger is a typical, healthy emotion that makes you feel:

attacked, duped, frustrated, invalidated, or subjected to unfair treatment.

It isn't always a "bad" emotion; in fact, it can occasionally be beneficial. For instance, getting upset about something can:

✓ help us figure out what issues or items are

harming us.

✓ inspire us to make changes, accomplish our objectives, and move on.

✓ give us a boost of energy as part of our fight or flight system to help us stay safe and defend ourselves in hazardous situations.

Most people will experience episodes of anger which feel manageable and don't have a big impact on their lives. Learning healthy ways to recognise, express and deal with anger is important for our mental and physical health.

Only when anger spirals out of control and threatens to hurt you or those around you does it become a problem. This may occur if you frequently act out your rage in a negative or destructive way.

Your total mental and physical health are being harmed by your anger.

Your default emotion, anger, takes over and prevents you from experiencing other emotions.

You still lack the capacity to express your rage in constructive ways.

How well you are able to recognize, manage, and express your emotions will determine how you will act when you're angry.

Not everyone has the same methods for expressing rage. For instance, some problematic methods of rage expression you may have picked up include:

✧ Outward displays of aggressiveness and violence,

such as yelling, cursing, slamming doors, punching or throwing objects, or acting violently or verbally threateningly toward others.

✧ Inward aggression includes telling yourself that you despise yourself, depriving yourself of necessities (such food or items that would make you happy), isolating yourself from the outside world, and engaging in self-harm.

Non-violent or passive aggression, including acting snarky or sullen without expressing any overt hostility or anger, avoiding eye contact, refusing to undertake duties, or executing them poorly on purpose, late, or at the last minute.

2. **Panic and anxiety attacks**

When we are worried, tense, or afraid, especially about events that are about to occur or that we believe may occur in the future, we experience anxiety.

Humans naturally experience anxiety when they perceive a threat to their safety. It is something we can feel, think about, and physically experience.

Most people occasionally experience anxiety. When dealing with difficult situations or changes, especially those that potentially have a significant impact on your life, anxiety is a common side effect.

If anxiety interferes with your capacity to live your life as completely as you would like, it may become a mental health issue. For instance, it might be an issue if:

- ✓ ☐your feelings of worry are very strong or linger for a long time.
- ✓ your fears or worries are out of proportion to the situation.
- ✓ You steer clear of circumstances that could make you feel anxious.
- ✓ Your anxieties are difficult to control or they feel really distressing.
- ✓ ☐you regularly experience symptoms of anxiety, which could include panic attacks.

You find it challenging to carry out daily activities or engage in enjoyable activities.

3. Bipolar illness

A mental health condition called bipolar disorder mostly affects your emotions. If you have bipolar disorder, you may occasionally experience the following:

◇ Manic or hypomanic episodes signify feeling ecstatic.

◇ Depressive episodes imply poor spirits.

◇ During manic or depressive episodes, there may be some psychotic symptoms.

These various sensations may be referred to as mood episodes or states.

The phrase "bipolar" describes the ability of your mood to alternate between two extremely unlike states, mania and depression. Bipolar disorder used to be referred to as manic depression in the past.

This ancient phrase may still occasionally be heard nowadays.

But misinterpretations of either phrase are possible. People may believe that it only refers to extreme mood swings between mania and depression. However, bipolar disorder is a lot more intricate than this.

Debilitating despair, mania, and anything in between are all possible during mood episodes. Your episodes could feel intense at times, while you might feel stable at others. And you might never go through particular emotional swings.

For instance, mania is not a symptom of bipolar disorder in everyone.

The phrase bipolar affective disorder may also be

used by some medical experts. An affective disorder is one that has a connection to mood or emotions.

4.   Thoughts of suicide

Suicide is the act of intentionally taking your own life.

Suicidal feelings can mean having abstract thoughts about ending your life or feeling that people would be better off without you. Or it can mean thinking about methods of suicide or making clear plans to take your own life.

If you are feeling suicidal, you might be scared or confused by these feelings. You may find the feelings overwhelming.

But you are not alone. Many people think about suicide at some point in their lifetime.

Suicidal thoughts and sentiments vary from person to person. You can feel helpless to handle the challenging emotions you are going through. You can feel more incapable of continuing to live the life you currently have than like you want to die.

These emotions could develop gradually or might evolve over time. And it's common to not understand why you feel this way.

How you might feel or think:

✓ hopeless, as if living were pointless.

✓ tearful and burdened by negative ideas.

✓ unimaginable suffering that you can't see ever ending.

✓ useless, unneeded, or unwanted by others.

✓ frantic, as though there is no other option.

✓ as if everyone would benefit from your absence.

✓ physically numb or cut off from your body.

✓ fascination with dying.

What you might encounter

✓ inadequate sleep, including waking up earlier than desired.

✓ changing appetite, gaining or losing weight.

✓ lack of self-care, as demonstrated by your lack of interest in maintaining your appearance.

✓ want to keep people at bay.

✓ drafting a will or donating property.

✓ difficulty communicating.

✓ Low self-esteem and self-hatred.

✓ impulses to injure oneself.

5. Trauma

Trauma is the term used to describe going through extremely stressful, frightful, or upsetting experiences. When we discuss psychological or emotional trauma, we may mean:

conditions or occurrences that traumatize us on how our experiences influence us.

Any age can be affected by traumatic experiences, which can have enduring effects. You can see any consequences right away or for a very long time because everyone's response to trauma is unique.

Trauma is a personal experience. Nobody else can understand how you feel about your personal experiences or whether they were upsetting for you. Even if you might go through the same things as someone else, you might react differently.

Any experience that leaves you feeling:

i. Frightened.

ii. under attack.

iii. Humiliated.

iv. Rejected.

v. Abandoned.

vi. Invalidated.

vii.Unsafe.

viii.   Unsupported.

ix. Trapped.

x. Ashamed.

xi. powerless.

Trauma may occur in the following ways:

✓ sporadic or continuous occurrences.

✓ being harmed directly.

✓ seeing someone else get hurt.

✓ living in a stressful environment.

✓ having a family or community that has experienced trauma.

If you've experienced harassment, bullying, or discrimination, your trauma may be related to aspects of your identity.

6. Self-harm

When you hurt yourself, you are using it as a coping mechanism for challenging emotions, traumatic memories, or overwhelming circumstances and experiences. Self-harm has been characterized by some as a technique to:

✓ express something that's challenging to describe.

✓ transform abstract ideas or emotions into

concrete manifestations.

- ✓ make physical agony out of emotional pain.

- ✓ lessen intense emotional reactions or thoughts.

- ✓ possess a sense of control.

- ✓ forget painful experiences.

- ✓ having a reliable source in their lives.

- ✓ punishing oneself for one's emotions and experiences.

- ✓ stop experiencing dissociative, numb, or apathy.

- ✓ give themselves an incentive to take good care of their bodies.

- ✓ communicate their suicidal emotions and thoughts without really killing themselves.

Although you could get a momentary sense of relief after self-harming, the root of your distress is unlikely to have vanished. Self-harm can exacerbate already challenging feelings and trigger new ones.

Even though there are always justifications for someone harming oneself, it's crucial to understand that there are risks involved. It can be difficult to stop self-harm after you've become accustomed to it.

7. Depression

Depression is a persistently depressed state that interferes with daily life.

Depression can, in its mildest form, be simply defined as feeling down. Although it doesn't prevent you from living a regular life, it makes everything more difficult and seem less important. Depression can be deadly at its worst since it can make you feel suicidal.

If you are diagnosed with depression, your level of

depression may be described as light, moderate, or severe. This indicates what sort of influence your symptoms are having on you presently, and what sort of treatment likely you're to be offered. Throughout a single episode of depression or over the course of several episodes, you could fluctuate between mild, moderate, and severe depression. Additionally, there are also distinct subtypes of depression:

✧ Depression that only manifests during a certain season or at a specific time of year is known as seasonal affective disorder (SAD).

✧ Dysthymia is a mild depression that persists for at least two years. also known as chronic depression or persistent depressive disorder.

✧ Depression that develops during pregnancy is

known as prenatal depression. This condition is also referred to as prenatal depression.

✧ Depression that develops within the first year of giving birth is known as postnatal depression (PND).

8. Recognizing voices

Hearing voices refers to hearing a voice (or several voices) when no one else is around, as well as hearing voices that other people nearby cannot hear. When hearing voices, different things happen to different people. Your voices might not bother you, and you might even find them reassuring and useful. They could annoy or occupy your attention. Or they might come out as obtrusive and scary.

Depending on the situation, you could feel differently about your voices. Depending on how you're feeling, what's happening in your life, or the voices you hear, this might be the case.

It's a frequent misconception that if you hear voices, you must be struggling with your mental health. However, evidence indicates that a large number of persons who hear voices do not have a mental health issue. It's a fairly typical human experience.

There are numerous causes of voice hearing. Here are a few examples:

✓ Voices while you drift off to sleep or awaken are possible when you're only partially asleep because your brain is still somewhat engaged in dreaming. Your name may be called or a brief statement made by the voice. Strange things can also come into view. When you are completely awake, these experiences normally come to an end.

✓ Having trouble sleeping can make you hear voices.

✓ Hunger - If you're really hungry, you might hear voices.

✓ A physical ailment may cause you to hear voices or see things that others cannot if your temperature is too high. Sometimes, hearing voices might be a symptom of other diseases. It's vital to discuss this with your doctor if you have concerns about it.

✓ You might hear voices if you're under a lot of

stress, anxiety, or worry.

Drugs: As a side effect of some prescription drugs or after using recreational drugs, you could hear or see things. These encounters could also occur when you are quitting medications.

Bereavement: If you recently lost a close friend or family member, you might hear them speaking to you or feel their presence. Many people have had this sensation, and some find it to be soothing.

Abuse or bullying - after experiencing either, you can begin hearing voices. This can involve listening to the abuser's voice. You may hear someone being nasty or threatening, or telling you to harm yourself.

Other traumatic experiences – you may hear voices as a result of other traumas, which can be related with post-traumatic stress disorder (PTSD) and with dissociative disorders.

Some people claim that hearing a voice is an element of their spiritual experiences. This may be a highly exceptional encounter that you feel helps you make sense of your life. Alternately, you can experience a ghostly voice in your head.

Unfortunately, there are some people who have incorrect ideas about what hearing voices entails. They might assume that you are dangerous or extremely ill if you are hearing voices. This can be upsetting, especially if those affected are close relatives, friends, or coworkers.

How we perceive or characterize our voices can vary depending on our culture or religion. Some experts might not be cognizant of cultural variations in voice understanding. Finding support that reflects your own perspective of your experiences may become more challenging as a result.

You could be reluctant to tell anybody about it or seek assistance if your friends, family, or larger community have unfavorable opinions about what it means to hear voices. Your stress levels could rise as a result, which would make the voices more upsetting.

It's critical to keep in mind that you're not by yourself. You are not required to put up with rude treatment from others.

9.   Mania and hypomania

Periods of excessive activity and excitement known as hypomania and mania can have a big impact on your daily life.

A shorter-term, milder kind of mania known as hypomania (usually a few days).

A more severe type that lasts longer is called mania (a week or more).

Mania and hypomania can be fun for certain people. Or you can find them to be extremely disturbing, unpleasant, or uncomfortable.

Hypomania lasts for a few days, and can feel more manageable than mania. It can nevertheless have a disruptive influence on your life and people may notice a change in your mood and demeanor. However, you may typically carry on with your normal activities without too much disruption.

Symptoms of hypomania can include:

✓ jubilant, joyful, or filled with well-being.

✓ extremely enthusiastic, as though you can't speak quickly enough.

✓ agitated and irritable.

✓ heightened lustfulness.

✓ easily distracted, like your mind is racing or you have trouble focusing.

Your behaviour may include:

✓ being active more than normal.

✓ speaking frequently or speaking swiftly.

✓ being incredibly friendly.

✓ sleeping very little.

✓ spending too much money.

✓ taking risks or letting go of social inhibitions.

A manic episode lasts for a week or longer and severely impairs your ability to carry out your regular daily tasks, frequently interrupting or ceasing them entirely. Extreme mania is extremely severe and frequently requires hospital treatment.

Any of the previously mentioned symptoms of hypomania can also be signs of mania.

You could feel:

✓ extremely bold or daring.

✓ like no one can damage you or touch you.

✓ believe you're more capable than usual of

performing both physical and mental chores.

✓ like you are able to perceive, hear, or comprehend things that others cannot.

Your actions can include:

✓ talking a lot, speaking hastily, or speaking in a way that is unclear to others.

✓ being really amiable.

✓ uttering or acting in an improper or uncharacteristic manner.

✓ either extremely little or no sleep.

✓ being impolite or combative.

✓ drug or alcohol abuse.

✓ spending a lot of money or in an uncommon way for you.

✓ lowering social reticence.

✓ putting your safety at grave danger.

Following a manic or hypomanic episode, you may:

✓ feeling extremely unhappy or ashamed of your behavior.

✓ having committed themselves or taken on duties that currently feel overwhelming.

✓ have few, if any, or no memories at all of what occurred while you were manic or hypomanic.

✓ feel exhausted and require a lot of rest and sleep.

You may notice that the episode is followed by a time of depression if you have hypomania or mania as part of another mental health issue, such as bipolar illness or schizoaffective disorder

CHAPTER 2

Postnatal depression and perinatal mental health

A "perinatal" mental health issue is one that you can have at any point during your pregnancy or up to a year after giving birth.

A major life event is becoming a parent. A variety of emotions are normal to feel both throughout pregnancy and after giving birth. However, if any challenging emotions start to significantly impact your daily life, you may be dealing with a perinatal mental health issue.

This could be a brand-new mental health issue or a

recurrence of an old one.

common perinatal mental health issues

1. Postpartum depression

Depression that occurs during or following pregnancy may also be referred to as:

when you are pregnant, antenatal depression

Postpartum depression (PND) affects new mothers around a year after giving birth.

Perinatal depression can occur at any point during a pregnancy or up to a year after giving birth.

The existence of postnatal depression is widely known. But less is known about the prevalence of prenatal depression and the possibility of both in some people.

Perinatal depression signs and symptoms

Symptoms of prenatal depression include:

✓ sad, upset, or emotional.

✓ anxious, restless, or irritable.

✓ guilt-ridden, unworthy, and self-critical

✓ void and numb.

✓ Isolated and unable to connect with others

✓ experiencing no joy in life or activities you typically find enjoyable.

✓ an illusion of reality.

✓ lack of self-esteem or confidence.

✓ Desperate and hopeless.

✓ unfriendly or uncaring toward your spouse.

✓ unfriendly or uncaring toward your child.

✓ suicidal thoughts.

If you have prenatal depression, you might experience any of the following:

✓ lapse in attention even when you have the opportunity.

✓ have trouble falling asleep.

✓ have less of an appetite.

✓ lack a desire for sex.

While pregnant and after becoming a parent, several of these experiences are frequent.

But if you're afraid that you might be going through perinatal depression, it's still crucial to bring them up with your doctor.

perinatal depression treatments

You might be given one of many therapies for prenatal depression.

To help you and your doctor decide on the best course of action for you, your doctor should go over these alternatives with you:

- ✧ Talking treatment.

- ✧ You might be offered cognitive behavioral therapy (CBT) or interpersonal therapy as talking therapies (IPT). These brief therapies are suggested for the treatment of depression.

- ✧ Medication.

- ✧ Most likely an antidepressant is what this is.

You can consult your doctor or a pharmacist if you have any questions regarding taking medication. We also provide details about using antidepressants when nursing or pregnant.

Combining medicine with talk therapy.

Some individuals discover that using medication makes them feel stable enough to benefit fully from talking therapy. Others, however, believe that using medication or talking therapy alone can be more beneficial.

In your location, there may occasionally be a large waiting list for talking treatments. In order to aid you while you wait for therapy, your doctor might prescribe an antidepressant.

perinatal depression self-care

Perinatal depression can be quite challenging, but

you can try the following measures to see if they work:

✓ Take care of yourself.

✓ As a parent, you may have high standards for yourself, but nobody can live up to their expectations all the time.

✓ If you find yourself feeling worse again or if you decide not to do something you had planned to, don't be hard on yourself. Be kind to yourself and try to treat yourself as you would a friend.

✓ Keep a mood journal.

✓ You'll be able to monitor any fluctuations in your mood and may discover that you have more pleasant days than you realize. This might also assist you in identifying any situations, persons, or activities that make you feel better or worse.

1. Maintain good hygiene.

It's simple for cleanliness to become less important when you're depressed. Smaller things, though, can have a significant impact on how you feel. For instance, even if you are at home, you could get dressed and take a shower.

Consult others who have had similar situations. Sometimes we may think we are the only ones who experience certain emotions. Peer support and advising groups are provided for people to discuss their ideas, emotions, and experiences.

2. pregnancy anxiety

It may be referred to as having anxiety during your pregnancy or right after giving delivery which are:

✧ pregnancy-related anxiety, also known as antenatal anxiety.

✧ postpartum anxiety, which usually occurs within the first year of giving baby.

✧ perinatal anxiety can occur at any moment throughout a pregnancy or for around a year following delivery.

Many individuals are aware that having a baby can lead to depression. However, a lot of people also experience anxiety throughout their pregnancies and right after giving birth. In actuality, having both symptoms at once is quite frequent.

prenatal anxiety's telltale signs and symptoms

Some of the typical prenatal anxiety symptoms and indicators include its consequences for your body.

The following are some common physical symptoms of prenatal anxiety:

✓ a queasy sensation in your stomach.

✓ feeling faint or disoriented.

✓ needles and threads.

✓ feeling unable to sit still or becoming restless.

✓ backache, aches and pains, or other discomforts.

✓ faster respiration.

✓ a pounding, rapid, or unsteady heartbeat

✓ hot flushes or perspiration

✓ having trouble falling asleep, even when you have the opportunity.

✓ teeth-grinding, especially at night.

✓ nausea (feeling sick) (feeling sick).

✓ using the restroom more or less frequently.

✓ modifications to your sex drive.

✓ experiencing panic attacks.

The following mental symptoms of prenatal anxiety are typical:

✓ feeling anxious, tense, or unable to unwind.

✓ a feeling of dread or apprehension of the worst.

✓ having the impression that time is passing more quickly or slowly.

✓ feeling that other people are staring at you and can tell that you're nervous.

✓ sense that you can't stop worrying or that if you stop worrying, horrible things will happen.

✓ Worrying about anxiety in general, such as worrying about potential panic episodes.

✓ needing constant confirmation from others or being concerned that others are upset or angry with you.

- ✓ apprehension that you're drifting from reality.
- ✓ worrying excessively about potential future events.

Rumination is the act of repeatedly reflecting on or thinking about unpleasant events or circumstances.

Depersonalization is the sensation of being detached from one's body or mind or of being watched by someone else.

Derealization is a sort of dissociation in which a person feels detached from or as if the world is not real.

perinatal anxiety treatments

You might be given one of many therapies for

prenatal anxiety.

To help you and your doctor decide on the best course of action for you, your doctor should go over these alternatives with you:

✓ Talking treatment.

✓ Cognitive behavioral therapy is the type of talking treatment for anxiety that you are most likely to receive (CBT).

✓ Additionally, your local mental health services might offer group or individual counseling for anxiety. To learn more about the options, chat with your doctor or get in touch with your neighborhood services.

self-help materials

You might be able to get online CBT programs

through your doctor. Or they might suggest self-help books to assist you in learning how to control your anxiety.

Medication

There are many different kinds of medications that can aid with anxiety management. You can consult your doctor or a pharmacist if you have any questions regarding taking medication. Discussing any worries regarding using medication during pregnancy or breast-feeding falls under this category. If you're concerned about having this conversation, visit our article on talking to your doctor.

Combining medicine with talk therapy

A verbal therapy and medicines may be prescribed to you. Taking medication often enables many people to feel stable enough to benefit fully from talking therapy. Others, however, believe that using medication or talking therapy alone can be more beneficial.

Your doctor could advise you to consider an alternative to treatment if there are huge waiting lists in your area for talking therapies. While you're waiting, you can use these to maintain your mental health.

perinatal anxiety self-care

When anxiety strikes, it can feel quite overpowering, making it difficult for you to handle interactions and daily chores.

Here are some suggestions about how to take care of yourself and cope:

To try to change your focus

Try to refocus your attention on something little, like the intricacies in a photograph or the texture of something you're wearing, if you're now experiencing anxiety over something.

Try to focus solely on this one thing if you can so that you can fully appreciate all the little intricacies. This may enable you to unwind for a while.

Learn to breathe properly.

You can reduce some of the physical symptoms of worry and promote relaxation by managing your breathing. An illustration of a breathing exercise

Try engaging in some exercise.

This can help you expend some of the anxiety you may be feeling as well as distract you from any thoughts that are causing you to feel nervous.

It's not necessary to participate in sports or visit the gym. You might wish to take a stroll or engage in some other physical activity around the house, like cleaning.

3.   **postpartum schizophrenia**

After giving delivery, a serious but uncommon mental health condition called postpartum psychosis can arise. It's also known as puerperal psychosis.

The symptoms of postpartum psychosis can be overpowering and terrifying, so it's critical to get care as soon as you can if you encounter them. But the majority of people totally recover with the correct assistance.

Postpartum psychosis symptoms and signs

Within a few weeks of giving birth, postpartum psychosis symptoms usually appear rather suddenly. Postpartum simply means following childbirth.

A combination of psychosis, depression, and mania are likely to be present if you have postpartum psychosis. Thus, you might experience the following widespread symptoms:

You could feel:

✓ elated or excitation.

✓ profoundly depressed.

✓ abrupt shifts in mood.

✓ disoriented or perplexed.

You could be:

✓ Restless.

✓ unable to go asleep, even when given the opportunity.

✓ not able to focus.

✓ experiencing hallucinations or other psychotic symptoms.

Hallucinations and delusions

You might suffer hallucinations and delusions as a result of psychosis.

Strong views that other people don't share are considered delusions. For instance, you might believe that:

✓ You're being tracked

✓ We are reading your ideas.

✓ You have enormous power and the capacity to affect events that are beyond your control.

✓ You possess unique insight or divine encounters.

Some delusions, such as the conviction that someone is attempting to seize control of or kill you, can be quite frightful. These kinds of delusions are frequently referred to as paranoia or paranoid thinking.

When you have hallucinations, you encounter things that those around you do not. As an illustration, hearing voices, experiencing hallucinations, and other strange sensations.

Postpartum psychosis causes

What specifically causes postpartum psychosis is not well understood.

However, there are some things that could increase your risk of getting it. For instance, if you possess

a history of mental health issues in the family, including postpartum psychosis

a schizophrenia or bipolar illness diagnosis

a difficult delivery or pregnancy

had a history of postpartum psychosis.

However, postpartum psychosis can occur even if you have never had a mental health issue before.

It's crucial to talk to your doctor or midwife about your mental health if you are more likely to experience postpartum psychosis. They may inspire ideas for future planning in your mind.

Postpartum psychosis treatments

You might be given one of many therapies for postpartum psychosis. To help you and your doctor decide on the best course of action for you, your doctor should go over these alternatives with you:

✧ Medication.

✧ To control your mood and psychotic symptoms,

your doctor is likely to prescribe an antipsychotic medication. They might also suggest an antidepressant to you.

✧ ECT: Your doctor might suggest electroconvulsive therapy if your symptoms are very severe and other therapies don't work (ECT).

The best approach to acquire the assistance you require may be determined by your doctor to be inpatient treatment. You ought to be admitted to a mother and baby unit (MBU), where you can stay with your child while receiving treatment, if that is possible.

Postpartum psychosis self-care

The most crucial thing to do if you are suffering from postpartum psychosis is to seek care. If you feel comfortable doing so, talk to a medical expert, such as your doctor or a psychiatrist.

You could chat to someone you trust about how you're feeling and ask for their support in obtaining help if you don't feel comfortable talking to a health professional about it.

After obtaining medical assistance, there are things you may do to take care of yourself while you recuperate, including:

i.   Sign up for a peer support group.

ii. Talking to other people can help even if you're feeling incredibly alone or like no one understands you.

iii. Sharing feelings and experiences with others who have gone through similar things is known as peer support.

iv. Understand your triggers.

v. Consider keeping a journal to record your feelings and life events. This may assist you in identifying trends or identifying factors that affect your mental health. Additionally, it can assist you in being more conscious of the kinds of events or emotions that might worsen your mood.

vi. This provides you the opportunity to recognize problems later on before they worsen and to seek assistance.

During pregnancy, managing existing mental health issues

It's a good idea to speak with your doctor as soon as you can if you become pregnant while struggling with a mental health issue. If you intend to get pregnant in the future, you can also talk to your doctor about your mental health.

You can maintain your mental health during pregnancy with the help of your doctor's planning assistance. They can also aid you in considering whether you might require additional support.

Managing mental health issues while having a newborn

It may be challenging to discuss how you're feeling honestly if you recently had a baby and are experiencing mental health issues. You may experience:

pressure to be joyful and ecstatic

as if you must constantly remain vigilant.

If you're having mental health problems, you could be concerned that you're a lousy parent.

concerned that if you are honest about how you are feeling, someone may take your baby away.

However, if you are struggling, it's crucial to understand that these feelings are not your fault. If you require assistance or support, you can ask for it.

It might be incredibly frightening if you have thoughts about hurting your child. It's crucial to keep in mind that having these ideas does not necessarily indicate that you want to hurt your child. You might be reluctant to discuss your emotions with anyone. However, the more you can express your emotions and talk about them, the sooner you will be able to receive support. Talking to a family member, friend, or a medical expert like your doctor or midwife can do this.

CHAPTER 3

symptoms of mental health issues

There are numerous potential causes for mental health issues. Although various people may be more severely impacted by specific things than others, it is likely that many people are affected by a complex combination of circumstances.

For instance, the following elements may contribute to a time of poor mental health:

- ✓ abuse, trauma, or neglect during childhood.
- ✓ loneliness or a lack of companionship.
- ✓ experiencing racism and other forms of discrimination.
- ✓ social exclusion, destitution, or debt.

✓ bereavement (losing someone close to you) (losing someone close to you).

✓ extreme or ongoing stress.

✓ having a persistent physical health issue.

✓ losing your work or being unemployed.

✓ housing issues or homelessness.

✓ becoming a person's long-term caregiver.

✓ abuse of drugs and alcohol.

✓ as an adult, using domestic violence, bullying, or another form of abuse.

✓ enduring a substantial trauma as an adult, such as participating in battle, experiencing a life-threatening situation, or becoming a victim of violent crime.

Your behavior and mood might be affected by physical factors, such as neurological conditions like epilepsy or head injuries. Before pursuing more treatment for a mental health issue, it's crucial to rule out any possible physical causes.

Although lifestyle issues like employment, nutrition, drugs, and lack of sleep can all have an impact on your mental health, there are frequently additional elements involved if you have a mental health issue.

According to research, some mental health issues may run in families. For instance, you are more likely to acquire schizophrenia yourself if you have a parent who has the disorder. However, no one is certain if this is due to our DNA or other variables, such as the environment in which we are raised or the manner in which we may have picked up our parents' ways of thinking, coping, and acting.

Although our genes may have a role in the onset of various mental health issues, no specific genes have been identified as being definite contributors to mental health issues.

And a lot of persons with mental health issues don't have any parents, kids, or other close relatives who also suffer from the same ailment.

The brain of a human being is incredibly intricate. Some study indicates that variations in specific brain chemicals may be related to mental health issues (such as serotonin and dopamine). However, nobody fully comprehends how or why. There is little evidence to support claims that someone's brain chemistry is the root of their mental health issues.

Even yet, you might find that some people continue

to utilize brain chemistry as an explanation for mental health issues, despite the lack of compelling evidence to support this claim.

Possible causes for this include:

Numerous studies have shown that some psychiatric medications can be useful in treating some of the symptoms of mental health problems, though not all medications have the same effects on different people. Some of these medications work by altering brain chemicals.

The notion that there can be a clear physical reason for challenging thoughts, feelings, and behaviors may make it feel easier to communicate openly about your experiences and ask for support. Mental health disorders can feel extremely personal and be difficult to explain.

Behavioral medicine

Therefore, healthy behavior intervention contributes to mental and physical health as well as the management of stress itself. With the rise in lifestyle diseases, therapeutic lifestyle change has become an important target for interventions for both physical and mental health promotion. Stress and mental health problems are closely related to unhealthy lifestyles that are risk factors for both mental and physical health.

Therapeutic lifestyle change (TLC) centered on stress reduction, diet, physical activity, and smoking cessation.

Training on stress management techniques

Since the interaction of the brain, mind, and body is implicated in the stress reaction, therapies based on mind-body medicine have been recommended as an effective means for controlling stress. Managing daily life stress and assisting recovery from adversity are vital for promoting mental health.

training on stress management techniques

Since the interaction of the brain, mind, and body is implicated in the stress reaction, therapies based on mind-body medicine have been recommended as an effective means for controlling stress. Managing daily life stress and assisting recovery from adversity are vital for promoting mental health.

In addition, if necessary, mindful listening techniques, forgiveness, and loving kindness meditation may be included.

Community involvement

In addition, social networks and social support may prevent mental health issues, such as mental health issues in children and cognitive decline, as well as promote wellbeing. Raising public awareness of mental health may be necessary to increase the acceptance of mental health care for the promotion and prevention of illnesses.

CHAPTER 4

Conclusion

It is important to pay attention to the idea that physical and mental health are interdependent. In fact, since mental and physical health are interdependent, measures that support mental health, such stress reduction, will also benefit physical health Along with treating mental diseases, psychiatrists now face major issues related to mental health promotion and illness prevention due to the growing interest in mental health and its management. Psychiatrists are most suited to handle these problems due to their extensive understanding of the bio-psycho-social elements that affect mental health and their diverse psychotherapy talents.

Many of the protective factors for good mental health are outside the purview of programs or systems in the mental health field created especially to promote or safeguard mental health. Throughout the course of a person's life, social, economic, and cultural elements like employment status, income, physical health, and experiences in childhood and adolescence all have a substantial impact on mental health. However, it has also been demonstrated that initiatives or programs meant to foster mental wellness and prevent mental ill-health have a significant impact and offer good value for the money spent.

Across the life course and in many situations, there are interventions to support mental health, foster mental resilience, and prevent mental illness.